JOHN LESLEY

BLUE-TONGUE LIZARD

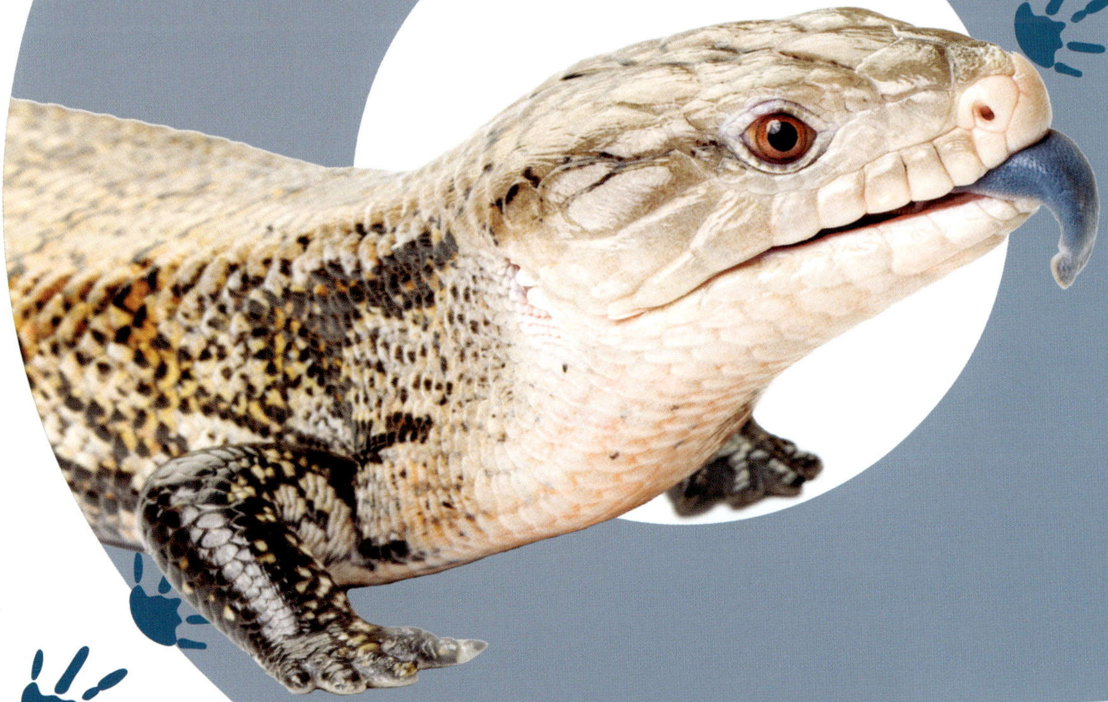

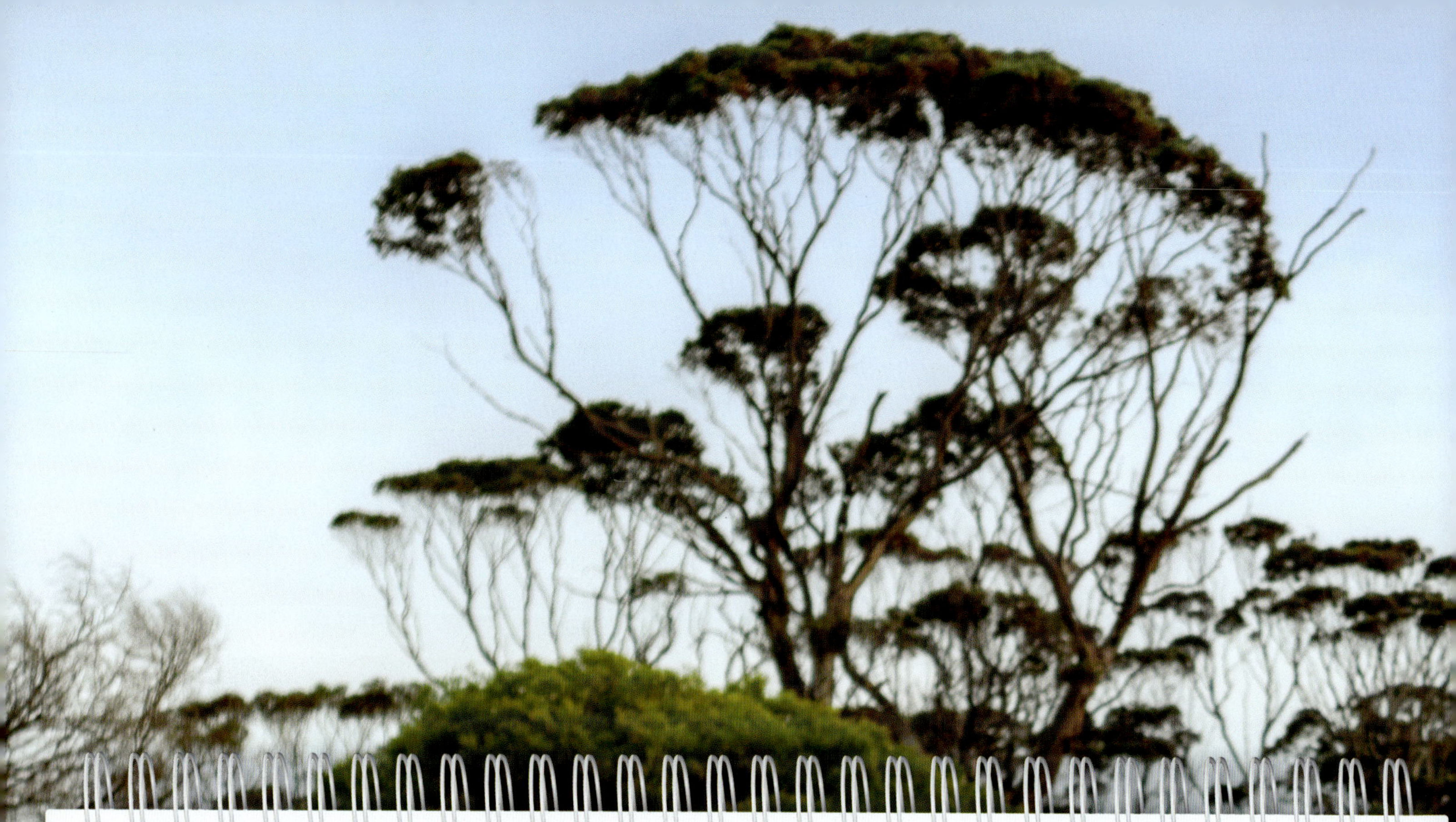

First Published 2025 by
Redback Publishing
Suite 6, 13a Narabang Way,
Belrose NSW 2085
Australia

www.redbackpublishing.com
orders@redbackpublishing.com

ISBN 978-1-761400-20-9 PBK

A catalogue record for this book is available from the National Library of Australia

Author: John Lesley
Editor: Caroline Thomas
Design: Redback Publishing

Original illustrations © Redback Publishing 2025
Originated by Redback Publishing

Printed and bound in Malaysia

Acknowledgements
We would like to thank © shutterstock for permission to reproduce their photographs

CONTENTS

WHAT IS A BLUE-TONGUE LIZARD?

Blue-tongue lizards are scale-covered reptiles that have been in Australia for millions of years. They are a type of skink. Skinks include the tiny, brown lizards that live in gardens.

Although they look like they might be little dinosaurs, lizards are not descended from them. The dinosaurs and the lizards have a common, ancient ancestor, but they both evolved separately.

Blue-tongue lizards are common in Australia, in both the bush and in suburban gardens. They are even seen walking along streets, often using gutters as a pathway to where they want to go.

In Australia, blue-tongue lizards are often just called 'blueys'.

4K UHD 3...2...1...1...2...3 00:35:02

They are not endangered, although being slow moving and often living in suburban areas makes them prey for domestic dogs.

Magpies dislike blue-tongue lizards and will swoop and attack if they see one on the ground.

BLUE-TONGUE LIZARD BASIC FACTS

SCIENTIFIC NAME

Tiliqua scincoides scincoides is the scientific name for the eastern blue-tongue lizard, (often called the common blue-tongue).

There is also a northern blue-tongue lizard that lives in Australia, and a Tanimbar blue-tongue lizard that is native to Indonesia.

COLOUR

The body has bands and patches of dark and light grey, with a creamy colour underneath on the belly and chin. There are stripes on the lower back and tail. The tongue is, of course, blue!

SKIN

Like most reptiles, blue-tongue lizards shed their skin regularly as they grow. The young lizards grow faster, so they need to shed their skin more often than they do as adults.

SIZE

Blue-tongue lizards can grow to half a metre in length and weigh up to a kilogram. They have a strong, fat tail.

SHAPE

The small legs sometimes make this lizard look like a snake. This appearance of slithering, together with the stripes on its back and tail, lead to it being killed by people who think it is a snake, before they have time to realise what it really is.

WHY IS THE TONGUE BLUE?

The blue-tongue is an adaptation that has evolved as a defence against predators. Blue is an unusual colour in the animal world, and its appearance is often a signal to predators that the animal they are considering eating is either poisonous or dangerous.

Blue poison dart frog

Blue-ringed octopus

The blue-tongue lizard may have evolved to look like a snake in both its body striping and in the way it sticks out its tongue as a warning. The blue colour will make a predator stop and take notice. If it cannot tell the difference, it may leave the lizard alone, just in case it is a venomous snake.

THE BLUE-TONGUE LIZARD BODY

ADAPTATIONS

An adaptation can be either a change in the body, or a new type of behaviour that animals have developed to allow them to survive better in their environment.

In lizards, all adaptations are probably based on a change in the animal's DNA and genes, rather than a change in behaviour that is passed on by learning from a parent.

LIVE BABIES

Blue-tongue lizards give birth to live babies. This means that there are no eggs that a predator can find and eat. The young lizards are born advanced enough to be able to run and look after themselves, giving them an advantage over other animals that need a parent to look after them for a long period of time.

TAIL

The tail can fall off if the blue-tongue lizard is really under serious threat of harm. The wriggling tail will then distract a predator, giving the lizard time to escape. The tail will grow back again, but it will be some months before it completely regenerates.

COLOURING

The grey stripes on a blue-tongue lizard's back make it look like a dangerous death adder snake, encouraging predators to leave it alone. Having very small legs also makes the blue-tongue lizard look like a snake. When the lizard is resting amongst leaves, stones and twigs, its colouring helps to camouflage it so that birds or animals that come near or fly over it cannot see it easily.

BLUE-TONGUE LIZARD HABITATS

COLD-BLOODED

Being a reptile, the blue-tongue lizard prefers warm areas. Reptiles are cold-blooded. This does not mean that they are always cold. They need to use the heat from the Sun to warm up their bodies to give them the energy to start moving around and looking for food.

Reptiles do not have the same automatic body heating and cooling mechanism that has been developed by mammals, like us. They need to use behavioural methods to warm up or cool down, such as basking in the Sun, or seeking the coolness of shade or water.

LANDSCAPES

Eastern blue-tongue lizards live in the southeast of Australia, particularly around Sydney and in the bushland of New South Wales. The northern blue-tongue lizard can survive in areas that are further north, hotter and drier. None of these lizards like to be in very cold, alpine areas. In the bush they live in forests and grasslands. Near towns and cities they live in gardens and reserves. In cold weather, blue-tongue lizards hide in a hollow log, or under leaves and branches on the ground.

Northern blue-tongue lizard

DANGER

Lawn mowers and garden tools are a danger to blue-tongue lizards, who will stay still and flatten themselves in the long grass, rather than run away when they hear and feel these implements coming near them. Gardeners need to take care to avoid a very unpleasant accident.

GARDENS

In a garden, blue-tongue lizards will look for shelter under any pile of rubbish or garden waste. They also like to crawl into pipes or empty garden pots.

BLUE-TONGUE LIZARD BEHAVIOUR

Blue-tongue lizards walk slowly with a side-to-side movement. They are not aggressive but will bite if they feel under threat. You can watch one from a distance in your garden without any fear that it will run up and attack.

They do not have any venom but, as with all reptiles, a bite from them can easily become badly infected. Their bite is very forceful and will be painful.

Like crocodiles, they hiss when they are annoyed, and they open their mouth to look more dangerous to a predator. They also flatten their bodies when really scared, to make themselves look bigger.

BLUE-TONGUE LIZARD LIFE CYCLE

BREEDING

Adult blue-tongue lizards are solitary, which means that they live alone. As the weather starts to warm up in spring, male and female blue-tongue lizards mate. The young start to grow inside the female, and she gives birth to them in the summer. There can be from one to ten baby lizards born at once, but there are also reports of many more being born at the same time.

NEWBORNS

Newborn babies are about fifteen centimetres long and can look after themselves immediately. After about three years, blue-tongue lizards are old enough to mate and reproduce.

A young blue-tongue lizard

PLACENTA

The blue-tongue lizard is remarkable because it does not lay eggs, like most other reptiles do. Instead, it gives birth to live baby lizards. The female develops a placenta, which is a structure that allows the babies to develop by being fed with nutrients from the mother's blood. The placenta normally only develops in placental mammals, so its presence in a lizard is very unusual.

LIFE SPAN

Eastern blue-tongues can live for a very long time in captivity. Some are known to have lived for twenty years.

BLUE-TONGUE LIZARD FOOD

Grasshopper

Blue-tongue lizards are omnivores. They like to eat plants and fruits, as well as insects, snails, slugs and bugs, as long as the food is close enough to the ground to be reached. They have flattened teeth used for crushing their food.

3...2...1...1...2...3 00:35:02

The blue-tongue lizard is not a climber, so it cannot reach food that is up high in a tree or bush. It does not have strong claws for holding onto tree trunks, although some lizards do climb small bushes.

Good gardeners like to encourage blue-tongue lizards into their gardens to help control the number of snails.

Blue-tongue lizards are very vulnerable to being poisoned by the bait that gardeners have spread around to control the slugs and snails. As the lizard eats the snail, it too becomes a victim. Just one more reason why natural control is better than scattering poison around a garden.

THREATS TO THE BLUE-TONGUE LIZARD

PREDATORS

Predators include the usual suspects, which are the feral dogs, cats and foxes. Since the blue-tongue lizard is so often found near houses, domestic dogs and cats are also a problem for them.

Cats will love to play with the lizard, tormenting it until they kill it.

In the bush, kookaburras and other birds of prey will eat blue-tongue lizards, as will snakes and large reptiles such as goannas.

TICKS

Blue-tongues can be plagued by ticks that get under their scales.

POISON

Eating poisoned snails and insects poses a threat to blue-tongue lizards.

CONSERVATION

As a native reptile, blue-tongue lizards are protected animals. They cannot be harmed or taken from the wild.

The IUCN Red List of Threatened Species lists blue-tongue lizards as having a stable population and being of 'Least Concern'. They are not under any threat of extinction.

PEOPLE AND THE BLUE-TONGUE LIZARD

HOUSES

If you leave a door to the garden open on a hot day, a blue-tongue lizard may wander inside to find a cool spot to hide. Slowly and carefully use a large piece of cardboard to direct it into a box. The lizard may thrash around a bit, so keep your hands out of the way. Take the box outside and release the lizard into a shady spot. Then close the door!

PETS

Blue-tongue lizards can be kept as pets under very special circumstances. If they are kept from a very young age, they become used to being handled gently. Their skin feels soft and smooth, and they sometimes like to sit in a hand for the warmth they get from it. Take care though, as they can bite very forcefully if they feel upset or scared. Keep them away from your face, eyes and ears, just in case!

CARS

Blue-tongue lizards often die on roads, run over by cars. The warm road surface is very attractive for them, and they go there to heat up in the Sun.

BLUE-TONGUE LIZARDS AS PETS

LICENCE

In most places in Australia, a blue-tongue lizard can be kept as a pet after applying for a special keeper licence. The lizard cannot be taken from the wild and should only ever be obtained from a source that breeds its own and has the appropriate licence. You are not allowed to take a native reptile from your own backyard and keep it as a pet. Remember that they can live for up to twenty years, so having a blue-tongue lizard for a pet is not a short-term exercise. It will be with you for a very long time, and it is illegal to release a pet reptile into the bush.

Ticks can infest the scales of reptiles

INFECTIONS

Blue-tongue lizards can be infected with intestinal worms and with ticks on their bodies. Find out how to best control these from your vet or from the source where you obtain your pet.

TANK

To keep a blue-tongue lizard, you will need a tank that is set up with a special heater, places it can hide and feel safe, and a cover to stop it escaping. Pet shops sell worms and grubs that can be given as food, or some people even feed their lizard on dog food. Take advice from the experts where you obtain your blue-tongue lizard, as feeding it the wrong sort of food can be fatal.

HANDLING

Your pet lizard can be handled gently but remember that they might bite. They do not like to be handled by cold hands and will be more comfortable if your hands are warm.

WHERE TO SEE A BLUE-TONGUE LIZARD

ZOOS

Most zoos and wildlife parks have reptile displays that include blue-tongue lizards. At one of these places you may be able to see the three different sorts of blue-tongue lizard all on the one visit. This is something that you will never be able to do if you are out in the bush. The different species of blue-tongues have evolved to live in their own regions and do not mix in the wild.

SUBURBS

On a quiet, hot day, you might be lucky enough to see a blue-tongue lizard walking through your garden or along the street outside.

PET SHOPS

Good pet shops that have blue-tongue lizards for sale will have all the appropriate licences. Ask about where they obtained their lizards before you buy from them.

BUSH

Bushwalkers rarely see blue-tongue lizards. This is because there are so many places for the lizard to hide. They will hear you coming, and may feel the vibrations of your feet on the ground.

SORTING ANIMALS INTO GROUPS

Biologists divide all living things around the world into groups. They call this process classification.

Here are the basic groups that describe all animals with backbones:

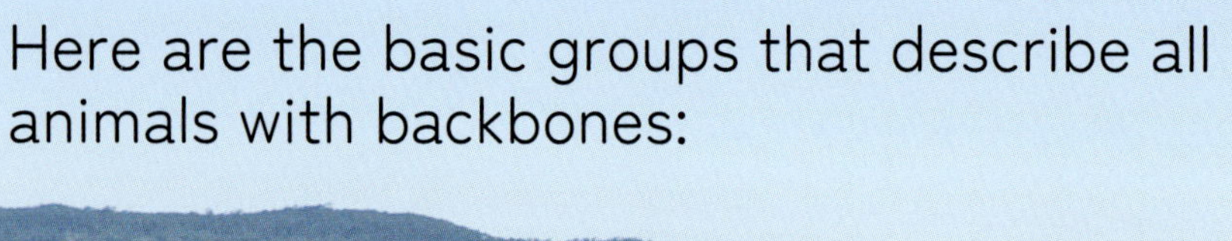

MAMMALS

Examples are dingoes and possums.

AMPHIBIANS

Examples are frogs and salamanders.

FISH

Examples are sharks and goldfish.

BIRDS

Examples are emus and penguins.

REPTILES

Examples are lizards and snakes.

HOMO SAPIENS

Humans have a scientific name and a position in the classification of animals. We are called *Homo sapiens*. These Latin words mean 'smart person'.

GLOSSARY

ancestor animal from which other animals descended

bait food left to kill or attract an animal

bird of prey bird that attacks animals for food

distract take attention away from something

fatal causing death

feral not native to an area

mechanism process to make something happen

native to has always lived in a certain area

omnivore eats plants and animals

skink small type of lizard

slithering sliding along without using legs

thrash about using fast movements of the body and limbs

tormenting causing distress and harm

venomous able to inject poison

4K UHD
00:35:02
4K UHD

INDEX